A View of Derry

Hugh Gallagher

GUILDHALL PRESS

Published in December 2008

Guildhall Press
Unit 15
Ráth Mór Business Park
Bligh's Lane
Derry BT48 0LZ
T: (028) 7136 4413 F: (028) 7137 2949
info@ghpress.com www.ghpress.com

Designed by Joe McAllister and Kevin Hippsley

ISBN 978 1 906271 17 6

A CIP record for this book is available from the British Library.

Guildhall Press gratefully acknowledges the financial support of the Arts Council of Northern Ireland as a principal funder under its Annual Support for Organisations Programme. We are also grateful to Derry City Council for Service Level Agreement support.

INTRODUCTION

The first camera I ever had was one that I won. By 'won' I mean I collected enough Peak Frean biscuit wrappers to get it, even though I had to persuade my mother to buy them. It took months and I was afraid the offer would be withdrawn. But from the moment I clapped eyes on the little object in Devine's shop window in Marlborough I had to have it. I was about nine years old then and had only taken photos with my father's Box Brownie camera occasionally; a roll of film stuck in it one day and I finished it off by trying to find out how the mirror system worked.

When I eventually got the mini camera, I rushed out to the top of Creggan and photographed everything in sight. The film took about six weeks to come back to the chemist shop I used and to my surprise, the prints were about one inch square – with a border! I was delighted.

My first serious attempt at photography was around 1985. I worked on a magazine while on an ACE scheme in Dove House. Frankie McMenamin got me the loan of a camera, but I couldn't afford to get the films developed. I worked with *Fingerpost* for several years, at times as an employee, at times as a volunteer, and have fond memories of the support and encouragement I got from Rose Gallacher, Catherine McGinty, Roy Arbuckle, Martina Doherty and others. Many of the photographs in this publication come from that period of my life and I acknowledge YES! Publications' support and contribution in making this book possible.

At the same time, I began to take photographs for *Cityview*, the Derry City football programme. Paddy 'Quiz' Doherty encouraged me and I travelled the length and breadth of Ireland annoying referees and unsettling goalkeepers, who didn't want me in their 'eye line'. Once, at Dalymount Park, my umbrella blew out onto the pitch during a match against Bohemians and the referee ordered me to retrieve it. I had no option so I ran out onto the pitch to a chorus of 'Spot, spot, spot the looney', from both sets of fans. Needless to say, I made sure I never brought an umbrella to a game again.

I still regard myself as an amateur and a historian, even though I have worked for both the *Derry Journal* and the *Derry News* for short periods. I met wonderful people along the way. In Siobhan McEleney, the *Derry Journal* had a gem of a human being. She is sadly missed. Then I encountered: Pat McArt, Bernie Mullan, Martin McGinley, Cecil McGill, Eugene Duffy, Jim McCafferty, John Conway, Eamonn MacDermott, John Gill, Artie Duffy, Mary McLaughlin, Willie Carson, Billy McLeod, Lorcan Doherty, Keith Moore, Trevor McBride, Margaret McLaughlin, Stephen Latimer, Phil Gamble, Joe Boland, Tom Heaney, Garbhan Downey, Jimmy Cadden, Martin McKeown and Seamus McKinney, all of whom helped or encouraged me in many ways.

A View of Derry is my first collection of photographs and it was a difficult task picking around 450 shots out of approximately 40,000 prints. Paul Hippsley, the manager and editor at Guildhall Press, promised to produce this book when I was employed there as a photographer for six months in 2008. With the help of Joe and Kevin and the Guildhall Press team, I hope we have produced a collection of images that not only capture my view of my home town but that evoke fond memories, bring a smile to your face, or even surprise you. If so, we have succeeded.

I would like to extend my thanks to Terry McCloskey, John Bryson, Joe McAllister, Kevin Hippsley, Paul Hippsley, Jenni Doherty, Declan Carlin, Frankie McMenamin, John Kelly, Conal McFeely and Joan Murray for their help in producing and launching this book.

Special thanks also to Geraldine O'Hara of the Local Strategy Partnership for the Derry City Council area for her encouragement and placement with Guildhall Press in 2008 which led to this publication.

I always regard myself as a spectator, someone who passes through life, not always getting involved, but standing back and observing as time goes by. Every year, around late Spring and early Summer, I head for a spot appropriately called Derryview in the Waterside. I never tire of the panorama I see from that vantage point. The landscape that is Derry lies before me and it seems to be endless in its changing shadows, vibrant colours and unique beauty.

Why, then, wouldn't you want to be a photographer?

Hugh Gallagher
Derry, December 2008

CONTENTS

A View of Derry

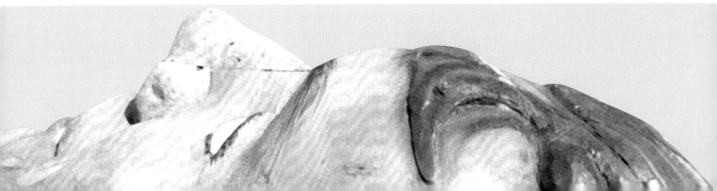

for my family

SPORTING PRIDE

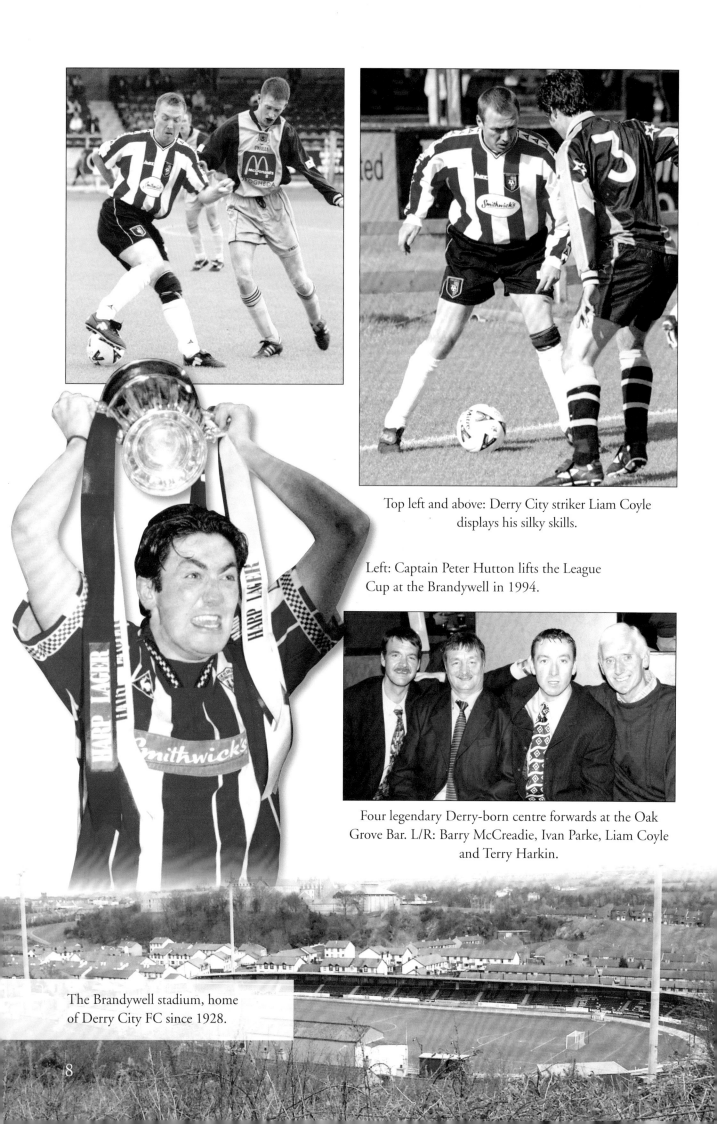

Top left and above: Derry City striker Liam Coyle displays his silky skills.

Left: Captain Peter Hutton lifts the League Cup at the Brandywell in 1994.

Four legendary Derry-born centre forwards at the Oak Grove Bar. L/R: Barry McCreadie, Ivan Parke, Liam Coyle and Terry Harkin.

The Brandywell stadium, home of Derry City FC since 1928.

Up for the cup at Dalymount Park in 1997. Derry City fans arrive in Dublin. Included are Dave Duggan, Joe Mahon, Terry McCloskey, Anne Corr and Tony Carlin.

City fans spot the photographer!

Derry City FC 'Old Boys', 2008. Front, L/R: Joe Loughlin (trainer), Donal O'Brien, Marty McCann, Gary Heaney, Joe Harkin and Tony O'Doherty. Back, L/R: Paul 'Storky' Carlyle, Harry McCourt, Stuart Gauld, Kevin 'Crack' McKeever, Declan Devine, Paul Curran, Noel Murray, Liam Coyle and Felix Healy. Also in photo is John Pio Doherty.

Derry City captain Peter Hutton is mobbed by Sean Hargan, Tommy Dunne and Liam Coyle after he scored against UCD to clinch the Premier Division title in 1997.

Referee Gerry Perry grimaces in pain after trapping his hand in the tombola machine when making the half-time draw at the Brandywell in 2000. Watching on, with 'absolute sympathy' for the poor referee, are Derry City fans Jim O'Donnell, Liam Gallagher and Marty Dunne.

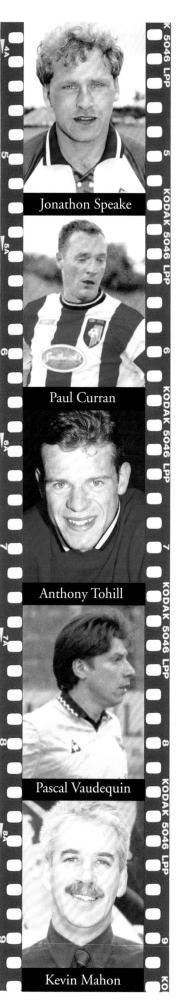

Jonathon Speake

Paul Curran

Anthony Tohill

Pascal Vaudequin

Kevin Mahon

Above: Jubilant Derry players after their victory in the League Cup Final in 2006. Below: Darren Kelly celebrates with Derry City fans in the Crescent Bar with the FAI Cup and League Cup trophies in 2006.

Brazilian superstar Ronaldinho scores against Derry City at the Brandywell.

John Pio Doherty and an ever-smiling Ronaldinho.

Marc Overmars is forced away from the Derry City goal by Eddie McCallion.

Famous Catalan team FC Barcelona line up at the Brandywell before their friendly match with Derry City in 2003.

Ball boys, and girl, prepare for a match at the Brandywell with club officials and volunteers.

Youngsters take part in a Football in the Community session at Derry City's Showgrounds training area.

David McCauley returns to Creggan in triumph after success at the Special Olympics World Games in Dublin in 2003.

Fanatical Derry fan Donovan McKeever and former Derry City player and manager Felix Healy at a testimonial game in 1998.

Derry City fans tackle their 'takeaways' at Carrickmacross on their way home from another long road trip.

Billy McLeod, sports photographer, 'at work' in the Brandywell.

Charlie Doherty, pictured at an FAI Cup game in Cork.

The famous Brandywell Pride in action!

THE FAT LADY SINGS TODAY

Harry McGarvey predicts that the day has arrived for Derry City to win the Premier Division title in 1997. Harry was proved right.

Lady stewards at the Brandywell make sure they will not go unnoticed in their fluorescent jackets.

England's 1966 World Cup winning custodian Gordon Banks passes on some tips to the St Joseph's Boys School goalkeeper on a visit in 2006.

Shauna McDevitt and Tracy Doherty wearing the Derry City home and away strips in 1997.

Anthony Tohill introduces President Mary McAleese to the Derry GAA team before the Ulster Football Final at Clones in 1998.

Derry's Seamus Downey, always first to the ball!

Joe Brolly in full flight at Clones in 1998.

Enda Muldoon in action at Celtic Park in 2007.

Paddy Bradley shields the ball at Celtic Park.

A determined Derry GAA team take the field to face Armagh against a backdrop of cheering fans in 2000.

Derry Minors celebrate their Ulster Football Championship success in 2002 at Clones.

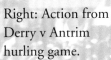

Right: Action from Derry v Antrim hurling game.

Left: A youthful Cormac McAnallen lifts the Ulster Minor Football Championship trophy for Tyrone in 1998.

Below: The joy of victory. Derry players celebrate the Ulster Minor Hurling Championship triumph in 2001.

Left and above: Ireland supporters celebrate in Shipquay Street during the World Cup in June 2002. Unfortunately, Ireland went out on penalties in the second round.

Local Glasgow Celtic fans with an unusual mascot in Waterloo Street before a televised Celtic v Rangers match.

CREGGAN V REST OF THE WORLD CHARITY MATCH IN 2008

FESTIVAL FUN

Below: Emmerdale star Lucy Pargeter, aka 'Chastity Dingle', poses with the staff of Ráth Mór's Rainbow Salon during the 2008 Revival Festival.

A happy group of '17th century riflemen' help launch Council's acclaimed book on the city's ancient cannon, *The Great Guns Like Thunder*, on the Walls with Council officer Elaine Griffin in 2008.

Just some of the large attendance at the book launch of *For You – Donovan* by Brendan McKeever at the Ráth Mór Revival Festival in 2008.

This brave juggler risked life, limb and digits performing in Guildhall Square at the city's Busking Festival.

Mayor Cathal Crumley with colourful costumed characters on board a Golden Link Festival float in 2000.

An enthusiastic troupe of Saint Patrick's Day revellers in 2008.

A sporty Charles 'Nucker' Tierney and friends at Creggan pitches.

Big smiles and much determination at these Creggan Féile fun races.

Happy faces at the Galliagh Festival.

A jam-packed Melmore Gardens street party.

Willie Barrett, Eamon MacManus and friends in the Grove Theatre Company ham it up in *Cinderella* pantomime at the Rialto.

Pipers stepping out in Shipquay Street during the Civic Parade.

Enjoying the rare Saint Patrick's Day sunshine in 2008.

HALLOWEEN FIREWORKS

'Heads you win!'

'Take that!' Magee students looking cool.

'Tally-ho, chaps!' Declan 'Biggles' McLaughlin.

'They'll be back!' Terminator Arnie and 'soldiers' on Halloween duty.

'You little devils!' Doherty's Bakery staff, Foyle Street.

'Girls just gotta have fun' at Greenwalk in Creggan.

It's a nautical theme for this gang at Beechwood.

This fetching juggler at Ballyarnett's Amelia Earhart Festival in 2007 is keeping his eye firmly on the ball!

30

This fire-eater at the Golden Link Festival is definitely warming up his audience!

Mayor Cathal Crumley and Miss Galliagh come a cropper at the Golden Link Festival when the poor horse takes a tumble. (Thankfully, everyone survived in one piece, including the horse.)

31

Golden Link Festival participants gather in the sun at the Shantallow shops.

Spectators at the inaugural Ráth Mór Revival Festival in 2007 enjoy the music on offer.

Above: All ready for fun and frolics at a Marieville Park street party. Below: Costumed revellers with Councillor Peter Anderson in the Bogside during the Gasyard Féile in 2002.

Beautifully attired Irish dancers pose on Derry's Walls on a break from Feis duties.

Martin and Mickey, hanging out at the Ráth Mór Revival Festival in 2007.

Consternation grows on this little one's face as she wonders where the rest of her tasty ice cream went!

The infamous DeLorean car comes 'back from the future' for the Mayor's Parade.

Actress Bronagh Gallagher meets some pupils from St John's PS on her visit to Creggan's Ráth Mór Centre.

A City in Change

The Bull Park is an oasis of green with the city and River Foyle stretching beyond. Taken from high above West End Park in 2008.

The original Bogside area in 2008 with the commercial city and Derry's Walls in the background.

From the top: Grangemore, Glenowen, St Joseph's Boys School, Beechwood Avenue, Ráth Mór, West End Park, Elmwood Terrace, Bishop Street, Bennett Street and the Abercorn Bar. Taken from Gobnascale in the Waterside.

The Bogside Inn and Westland Street, looking towards the Lone Moor Road and Marlborough area.

Above and below: Christ Church (1830) and Brooke Park. The statue of Sir Robert Ferguson MP (1796–1860) was moved here from the top of Shipquay Street in 1927.

40

Above and below: Brooke Park looking magical in frost and snow.

41

The Foyle Bridge (1983) from Ballyoan in the Waterside with Scalp Mountain and Donegal in the background.

Westway, Creggan, looking towards the Coolkeeragh/Maydown industrial area, Lough Foyle and Benevenagh Mountain, with the Foyle Bridge and Rosemount Factory in the mid-ground.

A view from Eastway Road with the Foyle Bridge and Coolkeeragh/Maydown in the background.

A striking view of Derry's Walls, St Columb's Cathedral (1633) in foreground and St Eugene's Cathedral (1873) against a backdrop of the sweeping Donegal hills.

Above: Lumen Christi College (the Light of Christ, 1997) on Bishop Street, previously St Columb's College (1879-1997), with Nazareth House in front and the City Cemetery in the background. Below: Derry City Council offices on Strand Road with the new Foyle pontoon in foreground.

Horse heaven at Glassagh behind Creggan. St Columb's College with its famous handball court and a roofless Star Factory can just be seen in the mid-ground.

The River Foyle winds its way through the city as, far above, a plane descends towards Eglinton Airport.

Above: In the distance, Upper and Lower Gobnascale as seen from Southway, with Lecky Road, Anne Street and the Showgrounds football pitch in the foreground. Ardfoyle and the Star Factory are in mid-picture.
Below: A scenic view of the city from Gobnascale with Craigavon Bridge, the winding River Foyle and the two cathedrals in view.

A night scene of Cullen's Amusements on the former Fort George site on Strand Road against a backdrop of the Donegal hills. Pennyburn Church is just visible behind the 'Big Wheel'.

Brandywell stadium floodlights loom through the fog with Ardfoyle houses on the skyline, as seen from the City Cemetery.

Above: The Translink Belfast train speeds past St Columb's Park in the Waterside. Below: The Guildhall (1912) and Waterside in winter sunlight from the top of the Tower Museum.

Above: The Strand Road from an unusual angle, high on Embassy Court in 1997. Note the large cruise liner at Derry quay.

Below: Ebrington Barracks (1841) in the Waterside, formerly a British military base.

Cuthbert Street, off Dunfield Terrace in the Waterside.

Barnewall Place, looking towards Margaret Street, off Spencer Road in the Waterside.

Local landmarks: Hassan's Forge, Lecky Road (top); The Boating Club (1868) off Strand Road, now a restaurant (bottom); the Clinic on Fanad Drive and the famous Black Hut, just over the border at Killea.

Mailey's Bluebell Bar in the 1980s and after refurbishment with its new Off Licence in the 1990s. Adjacent is the Gasyard Centre under construction.

Collon Bar patrons bid a fond farewell to the original Collon Bar on the Buncrana Road, demolished in 2003.

Demolition of Jackie Mullan's Bar and part of Hogg & Mitchell factory on Little James Street after serious fire damage in 1996.

Formerly Jackie Mullan's Bar, now Sister Sara's, at the corner of Sackville and Little James Streets, 2008.

This fine building on Frederick Street was originally the Cameo Dance Hall, became the Stardust, then St Eugene's Parish Hall.

The original Dodd's Bar on Foyle Road.

Above and below: An Siopa Gaelach at the top of Waterloo Street.

The Telstar Bar on Central Drive, Creggan.

Fading memories – Willie John's Bar, Foyle Street, once Patrick O'Kane's wholesale wine and spirit business. The El Greco Nite Club was on Sugarhouse Lane to the left of the picture, now the site of Foyleside car park.

Tyrconnell House Bar, Foyle Street, on the corner of Foyle Alley and opposite the former Metropole, now part of Foyleside car park.

The Carlisle Hotel on Carlisle Road, demolished in 2006, was at the top of the Breakneck Steps, now closed off by the 'developer'.

Above: The Magee Campus of the University of Ulster (1865).
Below: Interior of St Columb's Hall (1888) in New Market Street in 2008.

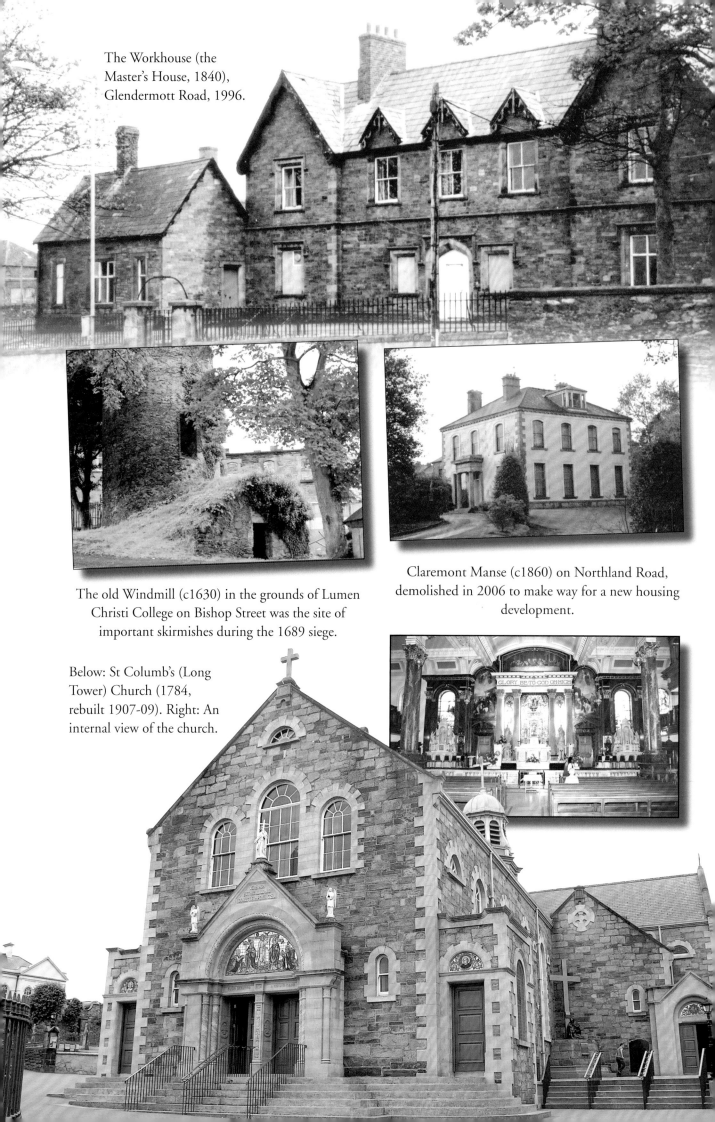

The Workhouse (the Master's House, 1840), Glendermott Road, 1996.

The old Windmill (c1630) in the grounds of Lumen Christi College on Bishop Street was the site of important skirmishes during the 1689 siege.

Claremont Manse (c1860) on Northland Road, demolished in 2006 to make way for a new housing development.

Below: St Columb's (Long Tower) Church (1784, rebuilt 1907-09). Right: An internal view of the church.

A fearless steeplejack cleans the spire of
St Columb's Cathedral.

The interior of St Columb's Cathedral

St Eugene's Cathedral with (above) the Parochial House. Opposite is a fine view of the ornate interior.

St Cecilia's Secondary School in Bligh's Lane, Creggan, was demolished in 2006 to make way for a new upgraded building on the same site.

Mothers Pride (Milanda) Bakery, on Glen Road/Northland Road, demolished in 2002 for a new housing development.

Dove Gardens in the Bogside was demolished in 2007 to make way for a new social housing scheme which got underway (below) in 2008.

The Trinity Hotel under construction on Strand Road in 1994 – now the Travelodge Hotel and Ice Wharf Bar.

An early morning explosion wrecked this takeaway next to the Alleyman's Bar on the Strand Road in 2004.

Linenhall Street/East Wall car park c1996 before construction of the Millennium Forum in 2001.

Left: The city Council's Rialto Theatre on Market Street c2000, with the Millennium Forum nearing completion in the background.

Below: The Rialto Theatre was demolished in 2005 and the site is now occupied by Primark.

Above and left: Foyleside Shopping Centre under construction at Orchard Street/Bridge Street c1994.

Below: Orchard House civil service office block takes shape on Water Street/Foyle Street corner c1991.

A surreal sight at the Diamond as the War Memorial statues are removed for repair and maintenance.

Above and below: Tillie & Henderson's Shirt Factory (1856–1895) on Abercorn Road/Foyle Road was demolished in 2003 after a series of devastating fires.

Above: Caught in a reflective moment – the image and the man.

Left: The derelict Star Shirt Factory (1900) on Foyle Road was later developed as an apartment complex.

Below: The imposing chimney stack on the site of the former Rocola Shirt Factory at Bligh's Lane was levelled in 2008. Sections were incorporated into the nearby refurbished Eastway Wall to preserve links with the area's industrial heritage.

The industrial past. The derelict former BSR factory premises (above and inset) on Eastway Road, Creggan.

The future is bright! The Ráth Mór Over 50s Club enjoying some of the many activities organised by Creggan Enterprises at the Ráth Mór Centre (below) on Eastway Road, Creggan.

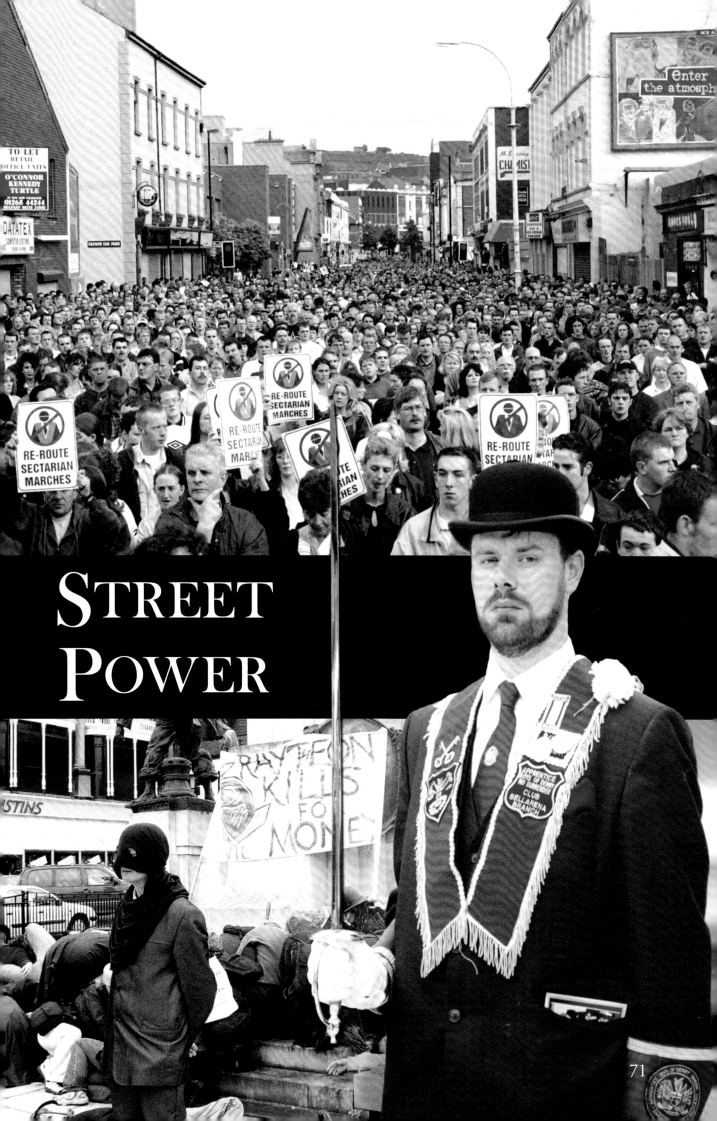

STREET
POWER

An Apprentice Boys march supporter erects a Union flag at Bishop Street.

A PSNI officer negotiates with a bandsman at the Diamond.

Donncha MacNiallais and Charles Lamberton of the Bogside Residents Group observe an Apprentice Boys march in Butcher Street through the RUC ranks.

Confrontation breaks out between bandsmen and nationalist protestors at the Diamond. This image made the front page of the *Irish News* in 1997.

An RUC support group looks on at Bishop Street.

An INLA Colour Party makes its way along Rossville Street in the Bogside.

A 32 County Sovereignty Colour Party in the City Cemetery.

Above: Former republican prisoners march along Southway during a Hunger Strike commemoration in 2006.

Left: A Sinn Féin Colour Party at an Easter Sunday parade in the cemetery.

Well-known local community activist Vinnie Coyle, on chair, chats with Martin McGuinness and Gerry Adams at the Easter Sunday commemoration in the City Cemetery c1996.

A protest against the British Army/RUC observation tower at Rosemount barracks. Protestors use balloons to hoist a banner at the post on Creggan Hill and local activist Dave Duggan of 'Toxic TV' contributes his own artistic input to the cause.

Rosemount tower campaigners Cecil and Marion Hutcheon seek a meeting with the Chief Constable Sir Hugh Orde to demand its removal.

The old Rosemount RUC and army barracks.

The tower protest moves to Waterloo Place.

Right: Hugh Gallagher, in glasses, picketing outside Derry Courthouse at the Bernadette Devlin trial in 1969. *(Courtesy of Martin Horsted)*

Protestors support striking workers at the United Technologies Automotive (UTA) premises on Eastway Road in 1997.

Community activists take a stand at Bishop Street in 2003 against funding cuts for community schemes.

The 'Raytheon 9' anti-war protestors march up Bishop Street to their trial in Derry Courthouse in 2008.

Eamonn McCann chats to an anti-Iraq war protestor at a Civil Rights march.

Playwright and activist Dave Duggan does a spoof broadcast on a picket at the Rialto against the appearance of comedian Bernard Manning.

Below: A Twelfth Parade peace campaigner caught in the act.

A Real Victims' march, organised by the group FAIR, passes through Shipquay Gate in 2001 with Andrew Hunter and Gregory Campbell in attendance.

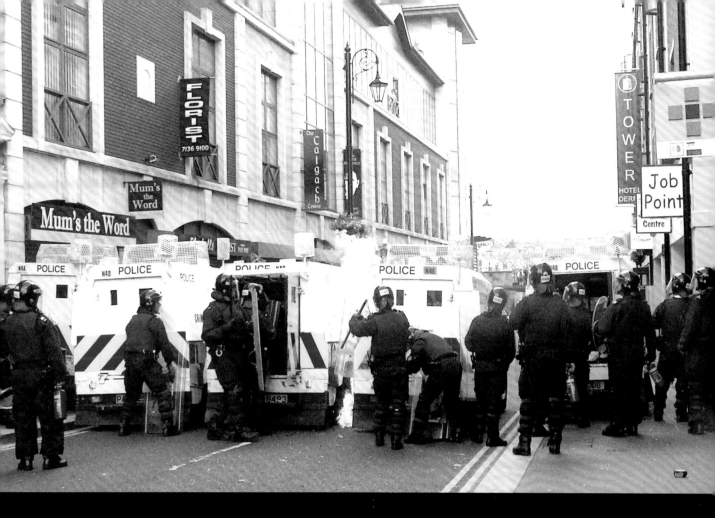

CULTURES IN CONFLICT

Hijacked vehicles burn in the Bogside in the shadow of the Apprentice Boys Hall and Derry's Walls. A large PEACE sign is visible through the smoke.

'Red' Jim Doherty and Niall Gallagher offer novel items for sale in William Street.

Petrol bomber in action at Guildhall Square/Foyle Street corner.

PSNI riot squad members at the ready at Ferryquay Gate.

Above and below: RUC riot squad members in Guildhall Square prepare for action.

Bonfire of the emotions.

Hijacked lorries at the top of Eastway Road in Creggan (right) and (below) on the Lecky Road flyover.

Bemused onlookers in William Street observe the aftermath of a fierce night's rioting.

A frustrated cyclist and his canine companion find their traditional route blocked at Butcher Street on the day of an Apprentice Boys march.

Local children turn this barricade in Little James Street into an impromptu playground.

SUNDAY REMEMBERED

The 2008 Bloody Sunday march passes down Brandywell Road.

Taoiseach Bertie Ahern and Mayor Martin Bradley join with others in solemn remembrance at the Bloody Sunday Memorial on Rossville Street in 1998.

US Senator Edward Kennedy and John Hume in the Bogside in 1998 with Bloody Sunday relatives Olive Bonner, Eileen Doherty-Green, Lawrence McElhinney, Kay Duddy, Ita McKinney, Mary Doherty, Mrs McKinney, Floyd Gilmour, Tony Doherty, Roslyn Doyle, Cecil Hutcheon, John Duddy, Geraldine Doherty and Mickey McKinney.

Bloody Sunday
march passes along
Lecky Road.

Kay Duddy, Kathleen Kelly and Helen Doherty make their way to the official commencement of the Saville Inquiry at the Guildhall in 1998.

The 14th Dalai Lama (meaning 'Ocean of Wisdom') visited Derry in October 2000 to meet some victims of the Troubles. L/R: Catherine McDaid, Kathleen Cooley, Linda Nash and Kay Duddy.

Peace campaigner Kim Phuc lays a wreath at the Bloody Sunday Memorial in 1999. Kim was the nine-year-old girl pictured in 1972 in one of the most iconic images of the Vietnam War, running naked down a road with her skin on fire from napalm dropped by US planes.

Local people gather to help in the making of the Bloody Sunday film featuring James Nesbitt in 2001.

Some of the local participants and actors who were involved in the making of the film *Bloody Sunday* in the city in 2001.

Vincent Coyle portrays his father 'Big' Vinnie who was chief steward at most of the Civil Rights marches in Derry during the Troubles.

James Nesbitt as Ivan Cooper along with George Downey.

Dr Raymond McClean.

Author Don Mullan as a priest.

James Hannigan and Jon McCourt.

General crowd scene and extras in *Bloody Sunday*.

Jane McNaught and Bernie Duddy in character during the filming of *Bloody Sunday*.

PICK AND MIX

SCENES FROM A HORSE FAIR

DAISYFIELD AND THE BRANDYWELL SHOWGROUNDS 2008

Above and below: Old Derry quay in the early 1990s.

The majestic Seabourn Pride cruise
liner docked at Queen's Quay in 1997.

Above: Madden's Tobacconist, once of Waterloo Place, is now long gone. Below: Tommy Maguire's fascinating shop at 35 Carlisle Road. Tommy is a specialist supplier of books, records (from wax cylinders through 78s to vinyl), postcards, coins, stamps and all manner of transport memorabilia.

St Patrick's Day 2008

Performers from Derry's Chinese community display traditional dragon costumes during the parade.

''hat's a cracker!'

Derry middleweight boxing sensation John Duddy leads the parade as Chief Marshal for the day.

Colmcille Pipe band members entertain the crowd in the Guildhall Square.

Stained Glass From Derry's Guildhall
Commemorating Victims of the Troubles

Stained Glass From Derry's Guildhall
Marking the City's Sacrifice in WWI

THE WALLED
CITY MARKET

101

CREGGAN COUNTRY PARK

Martin McGuinness joins in the fun for a charity event at the inaugural Gasyard Féile in 1993.

Contented workers take a break outside McCandless' Shirt Factory in Bishop Street.

President Bill Clinton and First Lady Hillary on a visit to Derry in 1995.

This enormous Gulliver effigy at Guildhall Square was later set afloat in the River Foyle as part of the Impact 92 celebrations.

The Great Escape! This unfortunate dog was somehow trapped in the War Memorial railings at the Diamond in 1997 and had to be rescued by the Fire Services.

'Look out behind you!', Creggan, 2003.

Dunree Beach from Dunree Fort, Donegal, 2008.

Congratulations! The Gallagher Clan Global Reunion in Letterkenny set a new Guinness World Record in September 2007 for the biggest number of people with the same surname attending a clan gathering. Some 1488 Gallaghers were counted by a Guinness Book of Records' official who declared that they had beaten the world record, set by the Jones family in Wales in 2006.

DERRY FACES

FAMILIAR FACES
IN DERRY PLACES...

Eddie Moran

Brendan Bradley

Paul McFadden

Charlie Nash

Clare McLaughlin

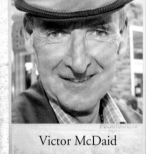

Victor McDaid

Willie Barrett

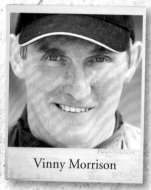

Vinny Morrison

Padraig MacDermott

Margaret McLaughlin

Ming Harkin

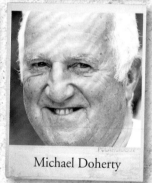

Michael Doherty

Margaret McKeever

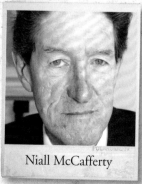

Niall McCafferty

Seamus Deane

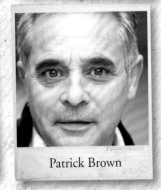

Patrick Brown

Margaret McGlinchey

Mary Gallagher

Hugh Gallagher (Snr)

Margaret Logue

Liam Gallagher

Eugene Gallagher

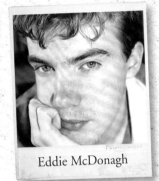

Eddie McDonagh

Michael Gallagher

Hugh 'Badger' McDaid

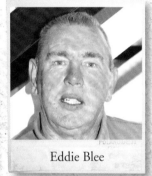

Eddie Blee

Eddie Harkin

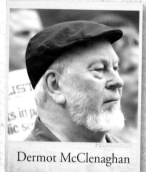

Dermot McClenaghan

Garry Donnelly

Lexie McFeeters

Frankie McMenamin

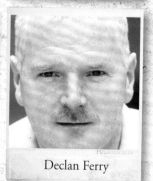

Declan Ferry

Charlie Ferry

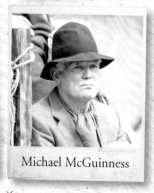

Michael McGuinness

Charlie McClaren

Gabriel Campbell

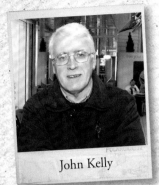
John Kelly

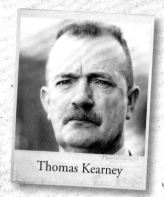
Thomas Kearney

Daniel Gillespie

Brendan Duffy

Brian Wight

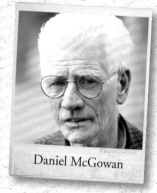
Daniel McGowan

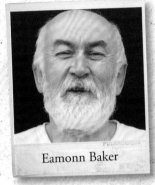
Eamonn Baker

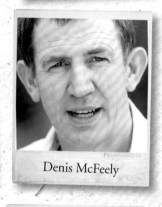
Denis McFeely

Peter McKane

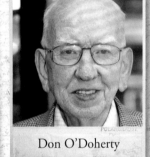
Don O'Doherty

Dougie Wood

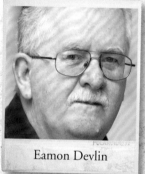
Eamon Devlin

Eamonn Deane

Eamon Melaugh

Eddie Mahon

Ellen Gallagher

Fay Coyle

Felix Healy

Fr George McLaughlin

Dessie Baker

Hugh O'Donnell

Fr Joe Carolan

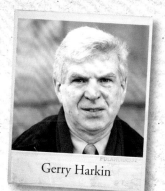

Gerry Harkin

Charlie McLaughlin

Paddy 'Bogside' Doherty

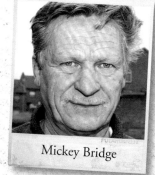

Mickey Bridge

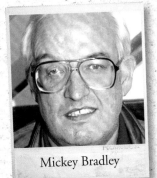

Mickey Bradley

Locky Morris

Liam Gallagher

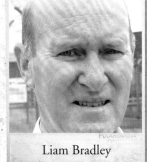

Liam Bradley

Laurnie Burke

John Breslin

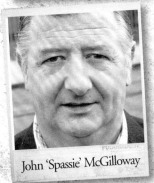

John 'Spassie' McGilloway

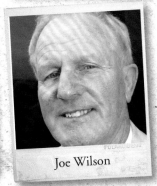

Joe Wilson

James Wray

Hugo Moran

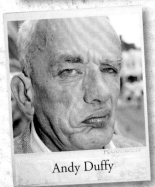

Andy Duffy

Heslin McDermott

Harry Hamilton

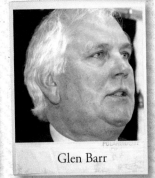

Glen Barr

Garvan O'Doherty

Garbhan Downey

Geraldine O'Hara

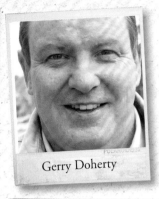
Gerry Doherty

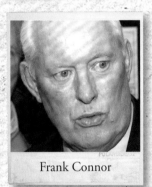
Frank Connor

Ann and John Starrs

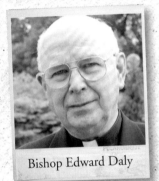
Bishop Edward Daly

The Quigley brothers

Ann McDonagh and John Duddy

Conal McFeely

Hugh McFeely with Lucy Pargeter

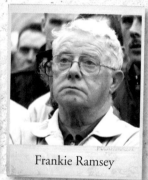
Frankie Ramsey

Tony, Trish, Stephen and Marcella Quigley

Nell McCafferty

Cormac Wilson

Johnny White

Barney McFadden and Gerry Adams

Donncha Mac Niallais

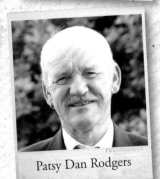
Patsy Dan Rodgers

Dodie McGuinness

Annie Courtney

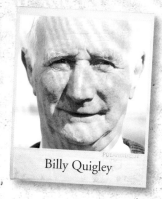

Barney Conaghan

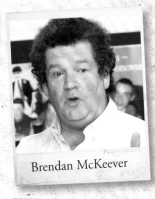

Billy Quigley

Brendan McKeever

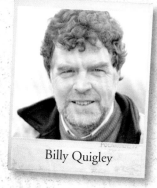

Ann and Mary McDonagh

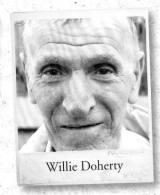

Billy Quigley

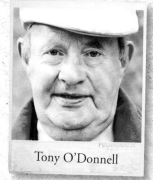

Willie Doherty

Tony O'Donnell

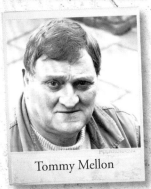

Tommy Mellon

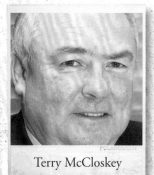

Terry McCloskey

'Smokey' Hasson

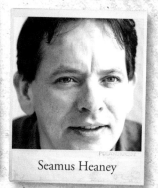

Seamus Heaney

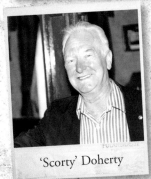

'Scorty' Doherty

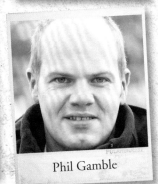

Phil Gamble

Peter Duffy

Gerry Newton

Paddy McGlinchey

Mustapha Oymak

Maureen Hetherington

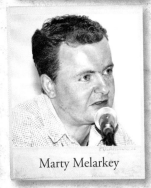

Marty Melarkey

FAMOUS FACES IN DERRY PLACES...

Alan Ball

Brian Friel

Bronagh Gallagher

Bruce Kent

Charlie Landsborough

Alex Ferguson

John Duddy

Hannah Shields

Kate Adie

Martin Bormann (Jr)

Jackie Fullerton

Wendy Austin

Seamus Ball

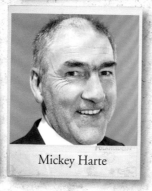
Mickey Harte

Michael Moore

Stephen Rea

PUBLIC FACES IN DERRY PLACES...

Pat 'The Cope' Gallagher

Seamus McKinney and Brian Cowen

Chris Patten

David Trimble

Arlene Foster

Mary Nelis

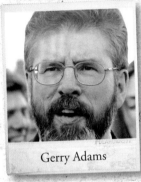
Gerry Adams

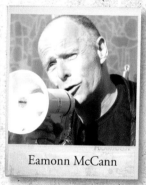
Eamonn McCann

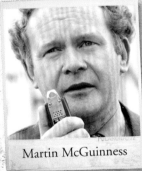
Martin McGuinness

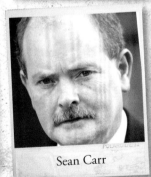
Sean Carr

Gregory Campbell

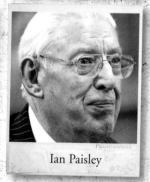
Ian Paisley

John Hume

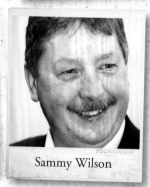
Sammy Wilson

Mark Durkan

Gerard Diver